d  e

h  i  j  k

 o  p

s  t  u

 y  z

This book belongs to:

NYLES & JOSEPH

22ND August 2003

Lots of Love
PAPA &
Darling xx

MY FIRST DICTIONARY

Illustrated by Jessica Stockham (Beehive Illustration)
Design by Design Principals, Warminster

This is a Parragon book
This edition published in 2003

Parragon
Queen Street House
4 Queen Street
BATH, BA1 1HE, UK

ISBN 1-40540-886-3
Printed in China

MY FIRST DICTIONARY

Written by Betty Root

p

Using this dictionary with your child

This colourful picture dictionary will be enjoyed by all young children. The very young will love to share it with an adult, talking about the lively pictures and giving names to those pictures they recognize.

Children who have just started to read will use the dictionary to understand the meanings of words and how to spell them. They may not know some words, so introducing them to children will extend and enrich both their spoken and written vocabulary.

The words in this dictionary are in alphabetical order. By using this book frequently, children will begin to remember where letters occur in the alphabet. This is a very useful skill. For each word there is an illustration, together with a simple definition and a sample sentence to help explain the meaning further. Care has been taken to ensure that the illustrations give the right clues to the sample sentences.

Children will want to return to this dictionary again and again because it is both attractive and satisfying. The joy of using the dictionary will help children to learn how to read many words and how to spell them. They will also learn that the world of words can be wonderful!

Betty Root

Aa Bb Cc Dd Ee
Ff Gg Hh Ii Jj
Kk Ll
Mm Nn
Oo Pp
Qq Rr

Contents

Ss Tt Uu Vv
Ww Xx Yy Zz

Aa

aeroplane

An aeroplane is a machine with wings. It flies in the sky.

People ride in aeroplanes to get to places quickly.

alphabet

The alphabet is the name for all the letters that we use to write words.

There are 26 letters in the alphabet. The first letter is a.

alligator

An alligator is a big long animal. It has a thick skin and sharp teeth.

Alligators use their long tails to swim in lakes and rivers.

angry

An angry person is someone who is upset or cross.

Baby Bear is angry because someone has eaten his food.

animal

An animal is something that is alive and can move around. Plants are not animals.

Monkeys, parrots, snakes and people are animals.

ankle

Your ankle is a part of your body. It is where your leg joins your foot.

Your ankle is a bone inside your leg.

apple

An apple is a round and juicy fruit. Apples grow on trees.

Apples can be red or green. Which ones do you like to eat?

asleep

When you are asleep you rest with your eyes shut. You do not know what is going on around you.

You are asleep at night in your bed.

astronaut

An astronaut is a man or woman who travels into outer space.

Some astronauts have walked on the Moon.

awake

You are awake when you are not asleep. Your eyes are open and you know what is going on around you.

Are you wide awake each morning?

Bb

baby

A baby is a very young child. Babies do not walk or talk, but they can make lots of noise.

A baby often sits in a high chair to eat.

ball

A ball is round and bounces up and down. You play games such as football and tennis with a ball.

You have to kick a ball hard.

balloon

A balloon is a small, thin bag. You can blow it up with air and make it bigger.

A balloon will blow away if you let go of it.

banana

A banana is a long fruit with a thick yellow skin. Bananas grow in bunches on trees.

You pull the skin off a banana to eat the fruit inside it.

basket
You use a basket to hold things. Some baskets are made from thin bendy wood.

My mum puts her shopping in a basket.

bat
A bat is a small animal with wings. It flies at night.

If you go into your garden when it is dark, you may see a bat.

A bat is a wooden stick. You use it to hit a ball.

You play baseball with a long thin bat.

bed
A bed is something that you sleep in. Your bed is usually in your bedroom.

Does your teddy sleep in your bed at night?

bee
A bee is a flying insect with six legs. Bees can sting you.

Some bees make honey for you to eat.

Bees visit colourful flowers in your garden.

belt
A belt is a long thin piece of leather or plastic. You wear it around your waist.

You wear a belt to stop your trousers from falling down.

bicycle

A bicycle is a machine that you ride on. It has two wheels that go round when you push on the pedals.

It is easy to fall off your bicycle when you first learn to ride it.

bite

To bite is to take hold of something with your teeth.

You bite an apple when you eat it.

big

Big means something that is not small. An elephant is a big animal.

If your jumper is too big, it will cover your hands.

blow

To blow is to push air out of your mouth.

You blow out the candles on your birthday cake.

bird

A bird is an animal with feathers and two wings. Most birds can fly. Birds lay eggs.

Small birds will come into your garden if you hang out nuts for them.

boat

You ride in a boat when you travel across water.

The Owl and the Pussycat had a pea-green boat.

book

A book is made from pieces of paper that are joined together. A story book has words and pictures in it.

Do you like to read a book at bedtime?

bread

Bread is a food made mainly from flour and water. You bake bread in an oven.

You can make toast with a slice of bread.

bottle

A bottle holds liquids such as fruit juice and sauces. Most bottles are made of glass or plastic.

Bottles can be lots of sizes and colours.

bridge

A bridge crosses over a river, a road or a railway. A bridge lets you get to the other side.

Cars drive over a bridge but boats go under it.

box

A box is a container with straight sides. It can be made from cardboard, plastic, wood or metal.

Do you put your toys away inside a box?

bucket

A bucket holds water and other things. It is made of metal or plastic and has a handle.

The bucket of milk has spilled over the floor.

a b c d e f g h i j k l m n o p q r s t u v w x y z

bulldozer

A bulldozer is a very big machine. It can move heavy stones and soil.

You see bulldozers at work on a building site.

butterfly

A butterfly is a flying insect. It has four coloured wings.

A butterfly sometimes spreads its wings in the sunshine.

button

A button is small and usually round. You have buttons to hold your clothes together.

You push a button into a hole or a loop on your shirt.

cake

A cake is made from flour, sugar, eggs and butter. You mix them together and bake them in an ove

A birthday cak has icing and candles on the top of it.

calculator

A calculator is a small counting machine. It can do sums very quickly.

A calculator is useful when you have to add up a lot of numbers.

camel

A camel is a large animal with one or two humps on its back. Camels live in hot places.

You can ride on a camel but it isn't very comfortable!

camera

You use a camera to take photographs. You put a special film in the camera.

Do you take a camera with you when you go on holiday?

canoe

A canoe is a small, thin-shaped boat. You use a paddle to move a canoe through water.

It is easy to fall out of a canoe, so you need to be careful.

carrot

A carrot is a long thin vegetable. It grows under the ground and you can eat it uncooked or cooked.

Rabbits like to eat carrots.

cat

A cat is a small furry animal. It has a long thin tail and pointed ears.

Do you have a pet cat in your home? What is its name?

caterpillar

A caterpillar is like a furry worm. Caterpillars change into butterflies and fly away.

Look for a caterpillar on a leaf in your garden.

a b c d e f g h i j k l m n o p q r s t u v w x y z

chair

A chair is something that you sit on. Most chairs have four legs and a back.

Goldilocks is sitting in Daddy Bear's big chair.

chicken

A chicken is a farm bird that does not fly. Mummy chickens lay eggs.

A mummy chicken is called a hen, and a daddy chicken is called a cockerel.

chocolate

Chocolate is a sweet food. It is made from cocoa and sugar.

Chocolate will go soft and sticky if you hold it in your hands.

clean

When something is clean it is not dirty.

You can make your face clean with a cloth and warm water.

climb

When you climb you use your hands and feet to go up something.

Do you like to climb up the climbing frame?

clock

A clock is a machine that tells what time it is. The clock's hands point to the right time.

An alarm clock makes a loud noise to wake you up.

clown

A clown is a person who dresses up and does funny tricks.

Clowns do silly things to make people laugh.

computer

A computer is a machine that stores lots of information. People use computers in shops, offices and schools.

You use a keyboard with a computer.

coat

You wear a coat on top of your clothes when you go outside.

A coat keeps you warm when it is cold.

cow

A cow is a large farm animal. Milk comes from mummy cows.

A daddy cow is called a bull.

cold

When something is cold it is not hot. It is cold when there is snow.

Do you get cold when you build a snowman?

crab

A crab is an animal with a hard shell. It has two claws and eight legs.

Have you ever seen a crab on the beach?

a b c d e f g h i j k l m n o p q r s t u v w x y z

crawl

To crawl is to move along on the ground by using your hands and knees.

Babies crawl before they can walk.

crocodile

A crocodile is a long animal. It has lots of sharp teeth and a very strong tail.

Crocodiles swim in rivers in hot countries.

cry

You cry when you are hurt or you feel sad.

Tears run down your face when you cry.

cucumber

A cucumber is a long thin vegetable. It has a green skin but is soft and white inside.

You can cut a cucumber into very thin slices.

cup

A cup is a small bowl with a handle. You put drinks such as tea or coffee into a cup.

A cup usually stands on a saucer.

cut

When you cut something you open or divide it. You can use a knife or scissors to cut.

Shall I cut the pizza into six slices?

Dd

dark

Dark means that it is not light.

You use a torch at night because it is dark outside.

desk

A desk is a table with drawers. A computer sometimes stands on a desk.

You sit at a desk to work.

dentist

A dentist is a person who looks after your teeth. A dentist can stop your tooth hurting.

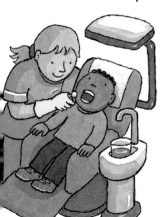

When you visit the dentist you sit in a big long chair.

dice

Dice have six sides with different numbers of dots on each side.

You throw dice when you play a board game.

dig

To dig is to make a hole in soil or sand. You can use a spade to dig.

A dog uses its paws to dig in the garden.

dinosaur

A dinosaur is a very large animal that lived a very long time ago. There are no dinosaurs alive today.

We know that some dinosaurs were as tall as big trees.

dirty

When something is dirty it is not clean.

If your shoes are covered in mud they are dirty.

dive

To dive is to jump into water head first. When you dive for the first time it is a bit scary.

Penguins can dive into very cold water.

doctor

A doctor is a person who looks after you when you are ill. Doctors try to make people feel better.

A doctor will visit you if you are in hospital.

dog

A dog is a furry animal with four legs. Many people keep dogs as pets.

Dogs are lots of different sizes and colours.

dolphin

A dolphin is an animal that lives in the sea. Dolphins are very clever and are often friendly.

If you are lucky you can watch dolphins jumping out of the sea.

drum

A drum is a musical instrument. You hit a drum with two sticks to make a noise.

I can make lots of noise when I play my drum.

donkey

A donkey is an animal that looks like a small horse. Donkeys have long ears.

Have you ever had a ride on a donkey at the seaside?

dry

Dry means not wet.

You stay dry if you use an umbrella in the rain.

dragon

A dragon is not a real animal. You can read about dragons in story books.

In stories, dragons usually breathe out fire.

duck

A duck is a bird that can swim and fly. It has special feet to help it swim.

I like to feed the ducks on the pond in the park.

a b c d e f g h i j k l m n o p q r s t u v w x y z

Ee

eagle

An eagle is a very large bird. Eagles hunt and eat mice and rabbits.

You will not see an eagle in your garden.

egg

A bird's egg has a hard shell. A baby bird starts to grow inside it. Birds, fish and insects lay eggs.

A baby chick has to break out of its egg.

ear

An ear is a part of your head. You have two ears and they help you to hear.

You use your ears to hear all the sounds around you.

elbow

An elbow is a hard bony part of your arm. It is where your arm bends.

You have to bend your elbows when you lift something heavy.

a b c d **e** f g h i j k l m n o p q r s t u v w x y z

elephant

An elephant is a very large animal. It has big floppy ears and lives in the jungle.

An elephant is the biggest animal that lives on land.

empty

Something that is empty has nothing inside it.

Your glass is empty when there is no more orange juice in it.

fairy

A fairy is not a real person but someone you read about in stories. Fairies have wings and are often very small.

A fairy waves her wand to do magic things.

envelope

An envelope is a paper covering for a letter. You put a letter inside it.

You write an address on an envelope and stick a stamp on it.

fat

Fat means big all round. A fat animal is not thin.

Some monsters are fat because they eat a lot of food.

a b c d e f g h i j k l m n o p q r s t u v w x y z

feather

A bird has lots of feathers all over its body. Feathers keep birds warm. They also help most birds to fly.

Some feathers have lots of very bright colours.

fish

A fish is an animal that lives in water. It can breathe under water. Fish have tails to help them swim.

Some people keep pet fish in a glass tank.

feet

Your feet are at the end of your legs. You stand and walk on your feet.

You have 10 toes altogether on your two feet.

flower

A flower is a part of a plant. Lots of flowers are brightly coloured and have a sweet smell.

You can give a bunch of flowers to someone you love.

finger

A finger is part of your hand. You have five fingers on each hand.

You can use your fingers to help you count up to 10.

fork

A fork has sharp points on one end and a long handle. You use a small fork to eat your food.

You use a big fork to dig in the garden.

fountain

A fountain shoots water up into the air. The water falls down and goes back inside it.

You may get wet if you stand very close to a fountain.

front

The front of something is the part that faces forwards. Your eyes are in the front of your head.

A car has bright lights on the front.

fox

A fox is a wild animal. A fox looks like a dog with a thick furry tail.

A fox might look for food in your garden at night.

fruit

A fruit grows on a bush or a tree. Apples and bananas are fruits. Many fruits are juicy and good to eat.

Which of these fruits do you like to eat?

frog

A frog is a small animal that can live in or out of water. Frogs like to live in ponds.

A frog can jump a long way into the air.

full

Something that is full has no space left inside it. You cannot put more into a full glass.

Your glass is full when the orange juice comes right to the top.

Gg

garage

A garage is a building where you keep your car.

Do you have a garage next to your home?

A garage is a place where you take a car to be mended. You can buy petrol at some garages.

A garage has a special machine to lift cars off the floor.

gate

A gate is a door in a fence or a wall. A gate can be made of wood or metal.

You can climb over some gates.

ghost

A ghost is not real. Some people think that dead people come back to visit us as ghosts.

Some ghosts are friendly but some are a bit scary.

giant

A giant is a very big person in a story book. Giants are not real people.

This giant is even taller than a house.

gorilla

A gorilla is a very big, strong animal. It has lots of hair on its body.

Gorillas live in the jungle in Africa.

giraffe

A giraffe is an animal with a very long neck and tall thin legs.

A giraffe can eat the leaves at the top of a tree.

grape

A grape is a small juicy fruit. You can eat grapes or use them to make wine.

Grapes grow in bunches.

goat

A goat is a hairy animal with horns on its head. Some goats make milk.

A mummy goat is called a nanny. A daddy goat is called a billy.

guinea pig

A guinea pig is a small furry animal with no tail. You can keep guinea pigs as pets.

Guinea pigs like to eat lettuce and carrots.

a b c d e f **g** h i j k l m n o p q r s t u v w x y z

Hh

hand

You have a hand at the end of each arm. Each hand has four fingers and a thumb.

You hold
a bat and a ball in your hands.

hat

You wear a hat on top of your head. A hat keeps your head warm and dry.

There are lots of kinds of hats. Who does the red hat belong to

happy

Happy means not sad. You are pleased about things when you feel happy.

You are happy if you win a medal on sports day.

head

Your head is joined to your body. Your eyes, nose and mouth are on your head.

Do you put a hat on your head when you go outside?

helicopter

A helicopter is a machine that flies. It has blades on the top that spin round. Helicopters do not have wings.

A helicopter can fly straight up into the air.

hot

Hot means not cold. When the sun shines you often feel hot.

If you eat very hot food you might burn your mouth.

hippopotamus

A hippopotamus is a very large animal. It has short legs. Hippopotamuses like to swim in muddy water.

A hippopotamus can open its mouth very wide.

house

A house is a place where people live. It is usually made of stone, bricks or wood.

Some houses have rooms on two or three floors.

horse

A horse is a large animal that can run fast. A baby horse is called a foal.

You can ride on a horse or use it to pull heavy things.

hungry

When you are hungry you want to eat food.

Do you feel hungry when it is lunch-time?

a b c d e f g h i j k l m n o p q r s t u v w x y z

Ii

ice

When water is very cold it turns into ice. Ice is cold and very hard.

You make cubes of ice in a freezer.

iron

An iron makes your clothes smooth and flat. You heat up an iron when you use it.

Never touch a hot iron because it will burn you!

ice cream

Ice cream is a cold, sweet food. It is made from frozen cream and sugar.

Which is your favourite kind of ice cream?

island

An island is a piece of land with water all around it.

You can travel all the way round an island in a boat.

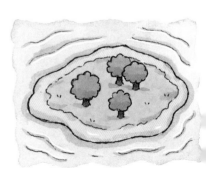

Jj

jar

A jar is made of glass or plastic. You keep foods and other things inside a jar.

You can put strawberry jam in a jar.

jelly

Jelly is a sweet food made from sugar, water and fruit. Most children love to eat jelly.

Jelly wobbles about on a plate.

jeans

Jeans are a kind of trousers. They are made from a blue material.

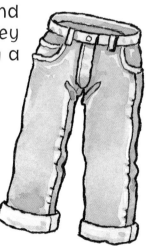

Both boys and girls like to wear jeans.

jellyfish

A jellyfish is an animal that lives in the sea. It has a soft body like jelly.

A jellyfish has lots of long thin legs.

jigsaw

A jigsaw is made of pieces of cardboard or wood. You join the pieces to make a picture.

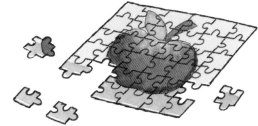

A jigsaw can have hundreds of different pieces.

jug

You put water and other liquids into a jug. A jug has a spout to pour the liquid out.

You pour drink from a jug into a glass.

jump

To jump is to leap into the air so that your feet do not touch the ground.

Do you like jumping on a trampoline?

kangaroo

A kangaroo is an animal that lives in Australia. It has very strong back legs so it can hop a long way.

A mummy kangaroo carries her baby in a special pocket called a pouch

key

You use a key to open a door that is locked. Keys are usually made of metal.

You have to turn a key in the lock to open the door.

kick

You kick a ball when you hit it hard with your foot.

How far can you kick a football?

knee

Your knee is part of your leg. It is where your leg bends.

Dancers have to bend their knees a lot.

kind

A kind person thinks of other people and helps them.

It is kind to give flowers to someone who is ill.

knife

You use a knife to cut something. A knife has a handle and a blade that is sharp on one side.

A knife can be dangerous so use it carefully.

kite

A kite is a toy that can fly in the air. It is joined to a very long piece of string.

Remember to hold the string tight when you fly your kite.

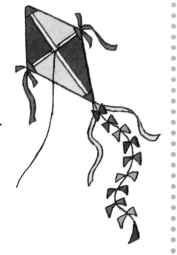

koala

A koala is a furry animal that lives in Australia. It has a large black nose and big round ears.

Koalas like to live in the trees and eat leaves.

Ll

ladder

A ladder is a set of steps. You use a ladder to get to high places.

The window cleaner has a ladder to reach the top windows.

lamp

A lamp gives off light. You can switch a lamp on and off.

Do you have a lamp next to your bed?

ladybird

A ladybird is a tiny insect that can fly. It is usually red with black spots.

How many spots can you count on this ladybird?

laugh

To laugh is to make a sound that shows you are happy.

Clowns make you laugh because they do funny things.

leaf

A leaf is the flat green part of a plant. Some trees lose their leaves in autumn and grow new ones in spring.

The leaves of an oak tree are bright green.

letter

You use letters to make words. There are 26 different letters. Together they make up the alphabet.

You use the letter 'j' to start the word 'jump'.

A letter is a piece of paper with words on it. You send a message in a letter.

You usually put a letter inside an envelope.

leg

Your leg joins your body to your feet. You use your legs to walk, run and climb.

You have two legs but many animals have four legs.

lemon

A lemon is a very sour yellow fruit. Lemons grow on trees in hot countries.

Lemonade is a drink that you make from lemons.

light

When it is light you can see what is around you. Light means not dark.

Is it light outside when you wake up in the morning?

a b c d e f g h i j k **l** m n o p q r s t u v w x y z

lion

A lion is a large fierce animal that lives in Africa. Lions are a kind of wild cat.

Lions are not friendly animals.

long

Long means not short. A giraffe uses its long neck to eat the leaves at the top of trees.

If your hair is very long it will touch your shoulders.

little

Something is little when it is not big. Little means the same as small.

A jumper that is too little does not fit you very well.

look

You use your eyes to look at things.

A pirate may look for ships to attack.

lizard

A lizard is a small animal with a long tail and four short legs.

Some lizards look like tiny crocodiles but they will not hurt you.

loud

A loud noise is easy to hear. If you play a drum you make a loud sound.

Do you put your fingers in your ears when you hear a loud noise?

Mm

magician

A magician is a person who does clever tricks. Magicians do magic for us.

Some magicians will make a rabbit come out of a hat.

map

A map is a drawing that shows you where places are. Some maps show you how to get to another city or town.

This map shows you some land with sea all around it.

make

You make something when you put lots of things together.

Do you like to make things with bricks?

match

A match is a small stick that makes a flame. You rub the thick end on something rough.

A matchbox usually has lots of matches inside it.

medal

A medal is a small circle of shiny metal. You may get a medal if you win a race or do something brave.

This shiny medal is on a colourful ribbon.

milk

Milk is a white liquid that comes from some animals. Cows, goats and many other animals feed milk to their babies.

Babies like to drink lots of milk.

mirror

A mirror is a special piece of glass. You can see yourself in a mirror.

You can look in a mirror and wave at yourself.

money

Money is metal coins or pieces of paper. You need money to buy things.

Do you keep your money in a purse?

monkey

A monkey is a wild animal with long arms and legs. Monkeys live in hot places.

A monkey uses its hands and feet to climb in the trees.

moon

The moon shines in the sky at night. It moves slowly around the Earth.

The moon is not always the same shape each night.

mouse

A mouse is a small furry animal with a long tail. Mice can live outside or inside your home.

A mouse can make its nest in a field of corn.

mug

A mug is a big cup. It does not have a saucer. People often drink tea or coffee out of mugs.

A mug often has pictures or writing on the outside.

neck

Your neck is the part of your body between your head and your shoulders.

Katie wears a red necklace around her neck.

mushroom

A mushroom is a small living thing that looks like a tiny umbrella. You can eat some mushrooms.

It is not safe to eat mushrooms that grow in woods.

nest

A nest is a home that birds and mice build. They build nests with twigs, grass and leaves.

Baby birds stay in a nest until they can fly.

abcdefghijklmnopqrstuvwxyz

net

A net has a long handle and a soft basket made from string. You use a net to catch fish.

Do you take a net when you go to the seaside?

nose

Your nose is on your face. You breathe through it. You also smell with your nose.

You use your nose to find out whether something smells good.

new

New means not old. New things have never been used or worn.

New shoes always look very shiny and clean.

number

A number tells you how many of something you have. You use numbers to count.

Can you see the number 5 in this picture?

newspaper

A newspaper has big pieces of paper that are folded in half. Writing and pictures are printed on the paper.

A newspaper tells you what is happening around the world.

nurse

A nurse looks after people who are ill. Most of the time a nurse works in a hospital.

Some nurses wear brightly coloured clothes.

open

Open means not shut. When a window is open the rain may come into your house.

If the front door is open you can walk into the house.

octopus

An octopus is an animal that lives in the sea. It has a soft body and eight arms.

An octopus uses its arms to swim quickly through the water.

orange

An orange is a round juicy fruit. You take off the thick orange skin and eat the juicy part inside.

Oranges keep you healthy and so they are good to eat.

old

Old is not new. Things that people keep for a long time are old. People who have lived for a long time are old.

Old shoes are not as shiny as new ones.

owl

An owl is a bird with big round eyes. It looks for food at night and catches mice, frogs and insects.

An owl makes a loud hooting sound at night.

Pp

paint

To paint is to put colours on a piece of paper or on walls. It is fun to paint a picture.

You use a big brush to paint the walls of a house.

Paint is a coloured liquid. It is often kept in small jars. You use paints and a brush to make a picture.

What colours are the paints in this picture?

panda

A panda is a very large black and white furry animal. Pandas live in China, and there are not many left in the world.

Pandas love to eat bamboo shoots.

parachute

A parachute is a big piece of material. It helps a person to fall slowly through the air.

A person who jumps out of a plane wears a parachute.

park

A park is a large area where people can walk and play. It has trees and flowers, and sometimes a playground.

Is there a park near your home?

parrot

A parrot is a bird with very bright feathers. Parrots usually live in warm countries.

You can teach some pet parrots to say words.

pea

A pea is a small green vegetable. Peas are round and they grow inside long thin pods.

You can eat peas uncooked or you can cook them.

peg

A peg is made of wood or plastic. You use pegs to fix clothes to a washing line.

If you do not use pegs your washing will blow away.

pencil

A pencil is a thin stick with black or coloured material inside it. You use a pencil to write and draw.

You can use a pencil to write a letter.

penguin

A penguin is a black and white bird that lives near the sea.

Penguins cannot fly but they can dive and swim.

Most penguins live in very cold, icy places.

a b c d e f g h i j k l m n o p q r s t u v w x y z

pie

A pie has pastry on the outside and meat or fruit in the middle. You bake a pie in the oven.

What is your favourite pie?

pig

A pig is a farm animal with a curly tail and short legs. A baby pig is called a piglet.

Many pigs are pink, but some are brown or black.

pilot

A pilot is a person who flies an aeroplane. Most pilots wear a uniform.

A pilot uses lots of instruments to fly an aeroplane safely.

pineapple

A pineapple is a yellow fruit. The skin is hard and prickly but the inside is juicy and sweet.

You cut off all the skin before you eat a pineapple.

pizza

Pizza is a food with bread at the bottom. It has different things on the top, such as cheese or ham.

Do you like cheese and tomato pizza?

plate

A plate is flat and round and you eat food from it. Plates come in many different sizes.

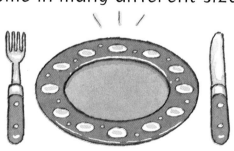

Some plates have bright colours and patterns on them.

potato

A potato is a vegetable that grows under the ground. It has a red or brown skin and is white on the inside.

You can make chips and crisps from potatoes.

pumpkin

A pumpkin is a large fruit with orange skin. Some people like to eat pumpkin pie.

You can make a special light out of a pumpkin.

present

You give a present to someone on a special day. A present is usually wrapped in pretty paper.

Do you get lots of presents on your birthday?

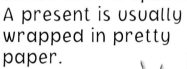

puppet

A puppet is a toy that you can move. Some puppets have strings. Some are like a glove that you wear.

You can make this puppet walk, run and dance.

puddle

A puddle is a little pool of water. There are lots of puddles when it rains.

You need to wear boots if you want to splash in puddles.

pyjamas

Pyjamas are trousers and a top that you wear in bed. You put on your pyjamas at bedtime.

What colour are your favourite pyjamas?

Qq

question

You ask a question when you want to find out about something. "What time is it?" is a question.

Why?

Children ask a lot of questions that begin with the word 'Why?'

quarter

When you share something into four parts of the same size, each part is a quarter.

Do you cut your apple into quarters?

quick

If you are quick, you do something fast. Quick means not slow.

A quick runner will often win a race.

queen

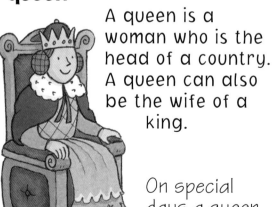

A queen is a woman who is the head of a country. A queen can also be the wife of a king.

On special days a queen wears a crown on her head.

quiet

If you are quiet you make no noise or only a tiny noise. Quiet means not loud.

Shh! You have to be quiet when a baby is asleep.

rabbit

A rabbit is a small furry animal with long ears. Most rabbits are wild but some are pets.

Rabbits like to eat lots of lettuce.

radio

You listen to music and talking on the radio. A radio is a small machine made of metal or plastic.

I listen to my favourite songs on the radio.

radiator

A radiator makes a room warm. A radiator is made of metal and is full of hot water. It is fixed to a wall.

The room is warm because the radiator is on.

rain

Rain is drops of water that fall from the sky. Rain comes from the clouds.

If you are outside in the rain you will get wet.

rainbow

A rainbow is a thick arch of different colours. You see it in the sky when the sun shines and it rains at the same time.

A rainbow has seven colours. Can you name all of them?

raspberry

A raspberry is a small red fruit. Raspberries grow on bushes.

A raspberry is very juicy and good to eat.

rat

A rat is an animal that looks like a large mouse. Most rats are brown or black. Some people keep rats as pets.

Rats often live in cities and towns.

read

To read is to look at words and know what they mean.

Do you like to sit in a big chair and read a story?

refrigerator

A refrigerator is a machine that keeps food cold. It is like a metal cupboard and has a motor. We often call it a fridge for short.

Food stays fresh and cool when you keep it in a refrigerator.

reindeer

A reindeer is a big deer with horns. It lives in cold countries. Reindeer horns are called antlers.

Father Christmas has lots of reindeer.

ring

A ring is a thin circle of metal that you wear on a finger. Men and women wear rings.

A ring with a bright stone sparkles.

roller blade

A roller blade is a boot with a row of wheels on the bottom. You can go very fast on roller blades.

You wear knee pads with your roller blades in case you fall over.

robot

A robot is a special machine. It can do some things that people do. Robots help to make cars in factories.

A toy robot can often walk and talk.

roof

A roof is the top part of a building. It covers the walls.

Birds like to sit on the roof of a house.

rocket

A rocket can fly straight up into space from the ground. A rocket sometimes takes people called astronauts into space.

A rocket makes a lot of noise when it leaves the ground.

ruler

A ruler is a flat piece of wood or plastic with marks on the side. You use a ruler to draw straight lines and measure things.

Can you draw a straight line without a ruler?

a b c d e f g h i j k l m n o p q r s t u v w x y z

Ss

sad

A sad person is not happy. People do not feel good when they are sad.

Some people cry when they feel sad.

sandal

A sandal is a shoe with straps. Sandals keep your feet cool in warm weather.

When you wear sandals you can see your toes.

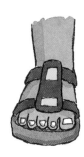

sail

A sail is a piece of material that is joined to a boat. Wind blows into the sail and makes the boat move.

Sails are often bright colours.

sandcastle

A sandcastle is a shape that you make with wet sand. You fill a bucket with sand and turn it upside down.

If you make a sandcastle on the beach the sea will wash it away later.

sandwich

A sandwich is two pieces of bread, with a food such as ham or cheese in the middle.

Do you take a cheese and tomato sandwich in your lunch box?

saw

A saw has a handle, a flat metal part and sharp teeth along one edge. You use it to cut wood and other materials.

You need a big saw to cut through a large piece of wood.

scales

You use scales to find out how heavy a person or a thing is.

When you make a cherry pie you weigh the cherries on the scales.

scarecrow

A scarecrow is a funny pretend person on a stick. Scarecrows scare the birds away from the farmer's seeds.

A scarecrow usually wears old clothes and a silly hat.

scarf

A scarf is a long piece of material that you wear around your neck. It keeps you warm.

Do you wear a scarf when you go out in the snow?

scissors

Scissors have two blades that are joined together. You use scissors to cut paper, hair and other things.

You can cut a piece of paper into pieces with scissors.

a b c d e f g h i j k l m n o p q r **s** t u v w x y z

screw

A screw is made of metal. It is like a thick nail but it is not smooth. A screw fixes two things together.

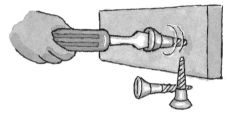

You use a screwdriver to turn a screw round and round.

seal

A seal is an animal that lives in the sea and on land. It has flippers to help it swim.

In very cold places seals live on the ice.

seatbelt

A seatbelt is a special strap in a car or a bus. It stops you being hurt if there is an accident.

When you sit in a car you must always fasten your seatbelt.

see-saw

A see-saw is a wooden or metal plank that two people sit on. Each person sits at one of the ends. When one person goes up, the other person comes down.

Is there a see-saw in a park near you?

shark

A shark is a big fierce fish. It has lots of sharp teeth and is not at all friendly.

Some sharks are very dangerous and can kill people.

sheep

A sheep is a farm animal with a woolly coat. We get wool, milk and meat from sheep.

A baby sheep is called a lamb.

a b c d e f g h i j k l m n o p q r s t u v w x y z

shell

A shell is a thin hard part on some animals. It fits around the bodies of animals such as crabs and snails.

People pick up shells from the beach and take them home.

shout

To shout is to call out very loudly. People often shout when they are cross.

Do you shout to your friends at playtime?

shirt

You wear a shirt on the top part of your body. A shirt often has buttons down the front.

People like to wear colourful shirts when the weather is hot.

shower

A shower sprays hot or cold water all over you. You stand under a shower to wash yourself.

People often have a shower before they go in a swimming pool.

shoe

A shoe keeps your foot warm and dry. Shoes come in lots of different colours and shapes.

How many pairs of shoes do you have?

shut

When something is shut it is not open. You cannot walk through a shut door.

Make sure the door is shut when you leave the house!

sink

The sink is the place in your kitchen where you do the washing-up. You fill a sink with water from the taps.

Do you wash the dirty dishes in the sink?

skyscraper

A skyscraper is a very tall building. Most skyscrapers are built in the middle of big cities.

Some skyscrapers are so tall that they seem to reach the clouds.

skeleton

A skeleton is all the joined-up bones in your body. People and lots of animals have a skeleton.

You have over 200 bones in your skeleton.

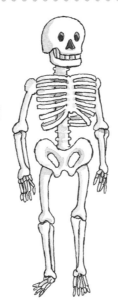

sleep

You sleep when you are tired. When you sleep your eyes close and your body is still.

The dog likes to sleep in a basket.

skip

To skip is to jump over a skipping rope. You skip as you move the rope under your feet.

Some children can skip very fast.

slide

A slide has a tall ladder and a long smooth part. You climb up the ladder and go down the long shiny slide.

I like the big slide in the park.

slow

Slow means not fast. A slow person does not move fast.

A tortoise is a very slow animal.

small

Small means not big. Small is the same as little.

I am small but my mum and dad are big.

snail

A snail is a small animal with a shell on its back. A snail moves very slowly.

Sometimes a snail puts its head into its shell and you cannot see it.

snake

A snake is an animal with a long thin body. It does not have any legs and it slides along the ground.

A snake can wind its body around the branch of a tree.

snowman

A snowman is a shape made of snow. When there is lots of snow you can push it together to build a snowman.

A snowman often wears a hat and a scarf, and has a carrot for his nose.

soap

You use soap to wash and to make things clean. You mix it with water. Soap often smells sweet.

You make bubbles when you wash your hands with soap and water.

a b c d e f g h i j k l m n o p q r s t u v w x y z

sock

You wear a sock on your foot. It is made of soft material. You put your socks on before you put your shoes on.

Some socks have bright colours and patterns on them.

spider

A spider is a small animal with eight legs. A spider makes a web to catch flies to eat.

Some people are scared of spiders, but most will not hurt you.

spade

A spade has a long thin handle and a flat part at one end. You use a big spade to dig in the garden.

At the beach you dig in the sand with a small spade.

spoon

A spoon has a long handle and a round part at one end. You use a spoon to eat foods such as soup ice cream, and cereals.

Spoons are made of metal, plastic or wood.

spaghetti

Spaghetti is a food that looks like long pieces of string. It is hard before you cook it, and goes soft when it is cooked.

It is not easy to eat spaghetti.

squirrel

A squirrel is a small furry animal with a long fat tail. It loves to eat nuts.

Most squirrels are grey but some are red.

stair

A stair is a step that you walk up. You have to climb the stairs to get to rooms at the top of a house.

At bedtime I climb each stair very slowly.

starfish

A starfish is an animal that lives in the sea. It has five arms and looks like a star.

A starfish does not look like a fish at all.

stamp

A stamp is a small piece of coloured paper. You stick a stamp on a letter or parcel before you post it.

You have to put a lot of stamps on a big heavy parcel.

story

A story tells you about things that have happened. Stories are not always true. You can read a story in a book.

The children listen to a story at the end of the day.

star

A star is a small bright light in the sky. You can see stars at night when it is dark.

There are too many stars in the sky to count them.

strawberry

A strawberry is a juicy red fruit. It is sweet to eat. You do not have to cook strawberries.

Strawberries grow on the ground so they are easy to pick.

a b c d e f g h i j k l m n o p q r s t u v w x y z

submarine

A submarine is a boat that can move under the sea. It can travel along the top of the sea as well.

A submarine can dive down very deep.

sun

The sun shines in the sky in the day. It keeps us warm and gives us light.

The sun is like a bright yellow ball in the sky.

swan

A swan is a large bird with a long neck. It lives in rivers and lakes. Swans have big strong wings.

I like feeding bread to the swans on the river.

sweep

You use a brush to sweep a floor. When you sweep you make something clean and tidy.

I sweep the leaves when they fall off the trees.

swing

A swing has two thick pieces of rope or metal, and a piece of wood for the seat. You sit on a swing and make it move backwards and forwards.

If you go very high on a swing remember to hold on tightly.

switch

A switch is what you use to turn things on and off. You press a switch to turn on a radio or a light.

The light comes on when you press the switch.

Tt

table

A table has a flat top and usually four legs. You sit at a table to eat your meals.

What can you see on top of this table?

tail

A tail is the long thin part at the back of some animals. A mouse has a long tail. A pig has a curly tail.

A dog wags its tail when it is happy.

tadpole

A tadpole is a baby frog. It lives in water and has no legs at first.

When a tadpole grows legs and loses its tail, it turns into a frog.

teddy bear

A teddy bear is a furry toy. Teddy bears can be small or large, and they are all cuddly.

My teddy bear sleeps in my bed at night.

a b c d e f g h i j k l m n o p q r s **t** u v w x y z

teeth

Your teeth are the hard white parts in your mouth. You use your teeth to eat your food.

You should brush your teeth twice each day.

telephone

A telephone is a machine that lets you talk to people who are in another place.

When a telephone rings you know that someone wants to talk to you.

telescope

A telescope lets you see things that are a long way away. It has a long thin tube that you look through.

The stars look bigger when you see them through a telescope.

television

A television is a machine that brings you pictures and sounds from other places.

Which programme do you like to watch on your television?

tent

A tent is a little house made of soft material.

You can sleep outside in a tent.

thermometer

A thermometer tells you how hot or cold something is. A nurse or doctor may put it in your mouth if you are ill.

A thermometer tells you when a sick person is very hot.

thin

Thin means not fat. A pencil is thin.

The monster has long thin arms and legs.

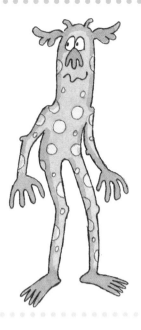

toad

A toad is like a big frog. A toad crawls about on land, but a frog jumps.

If you touch a toad you can feel the bumps under its skin.

thumb

A thumb is the thick short finger on your hand. You have two thumbs.

My big brother sticks up his thumb when he wants to say "Yes!"

toe

You have five toes on the end of each foot. Your toes are all different sizes.

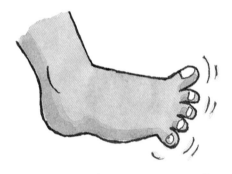

Can you wiggle your toes?

tiger

A tiger is a large wild animal. It is like a big cat with an orange coat and black stripes.

A tiger is a strong and fierce animal.

tomato

A tomato is a soft round fruit. Tomatoes are red and they grow on bushes.

You can cut up a tomato and eat it in a salad.

a b c d e f g h i j k l m n o p q r s t u v w x y z

tongue

Your tongue is the soft pink part inside your mouth. Your tongue helps you to taste your food.

It's a bit rude to stick out your tongue!

towel

A towel is a cloth that you use to dry yourself. Towels are soft and colourful.

Do you have a favourite towel in your home?

toothbrush

A toothbrush has a handle and a small brush at one end. You use it to clean your teeth.

You put toothpaste on the end of your toothbrush.

toy

A toy is a thing that a child plays with. Dolls, bricks, train sets and jack-in-the-boxes are toys.

You often keep toys in a toybox.

top

The top is the highest part of a thing. If you walk to the top of the hill you get to the highest point.

She put the box on top of the tall cupboard.

tractor

A tractor is a farm machine with big wheels at the back. It pulls heavy loads and other machines.

The farmer drives his tractor across the field.

train

A train moves along a railway track. It has an engine that pulls coaches. People ride in a train from place to place.

A train goes fast so you get to places quickly.

trumpet

A trumpet is a musical instrument. It is made of metal. You blow into one end and sounds come out of the other end.

When you play the trumpet you have to blow hard.

tree

A tree is a tall plant. It has a thick middle part that is made of wood. Many trees have green leaves.

You can pick red apples from this apple tree.

trunk

A trunk is the long nose on an elephant. Elephants use their trunks to pick up food and water.

Elephants spray water out of their trunks.

trousers

You wear trousers on the bottom part of your body. Trousers cover your legs and reach down to your feet.

It is easier to pull on your trousers if you sit down.

turtle

A turtle looks like a big tortoise. It can live on land or in water.

A mummy turtle often lays her eggs in the sand.

umbrella

An umbrella stops you getting wet when it rains. You hold an umbrella over your head.

Some umbrellas have pictures on them.

vacuum cleaner

A vacuum cleaner sucks up dirt from floors and carpets. It saves you a lot of hard work.

You can clean up quickly if you use a vacuum cleaner.

unicorn

A unicorn is not a real animal. It is a make-believe animal that looks like a horse with a horn on its head.

You read about unicorns in fairy stories.

vase

You fill a vase with water and put flowers in it. A vase is usually tall and thin.

When you pick flowers from the garden you put them in a vase.

vegetable

A vegetable is a part of a plant that you can eat. Potatoes and carrots are vegetables.

Which vegetables do you like to eat?

vet

A vet is a special doctor who looks after animals. You can take your pet animals to a vet.

If your pet cat is ill you take it to a vet.

violin

A violin is a musical instrument. It has four strings and you play it with a long stick called a bow.

You hold a violin under your chin to play it.

wash

You wash something to make it clean. You wash your hands with soap and water to make them clean.

Do you help to wash the car when it's dirty?

water

Water is the clear liquid in rivers and seas. Water falls out of the sky as rain.

Water from the tap has no taste, but water from the sea is salty.

wet

When something is wet it is covered with water. It is not dry.

You get very wet in the rain if you forget your umbrella.

witch

A witch is a make-believe person in a story. Witches wear tall pointed hats and fly on broomsticks.

A witch often has a black cat with her.

wheel

All wheels are round and they turn. Wheels help cars, bicycles and tractors to move along.

A tractor has big wheels but a buggy has small ones.

wizard

A wizard is a make-believe person who does magic. You read about wizards in stories.

A wizard can do clever magic tricks.

wind

Wind is air that moves fast. A strong wind blows things about.

The wind helps to dry the wet clothes.

write

You put letters or words onto paper when you write. You can write with a pencil or a pen.

She likes to write in her diary every day.

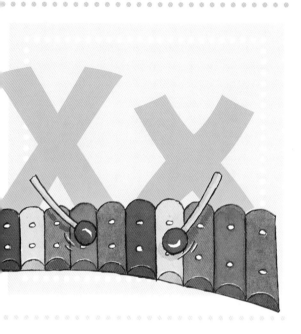

x-ray

An x-ray is a special photograph. It lets a doctor see inside your body. You have to go to a hospital for an x-ray.

An x-ray shows if a bone is broken.

yawn

You open your mouth wide when you yawn. This lets in lots of air. People yawn when they are tired.

You yawn when you are ready to go to bed.

xylophone

A xylophone is a musical instrument. It has rows of bars that you hit with two small hammers.

Can you play a song on a xylophone?

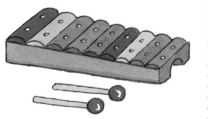

year

A year is the time it takes for the Earth to move around the Sun. There are 12 months, or just over 365 days, in a year.

A calendar shows you how many days are in a year.

a b c d e f g h i j k l m n o p q r s t u v w x y z

yoghurt

Yoghurt is a creamy food that is made from milk. Sugar and fruit can be added to yoghurt.

Cherry yoghurt is pink and tastes sweet.

young

You are young if you were born a short time ago. Young means not old.

A baby is a young person.

yo-yo

A yo-yo is a round toy on a long piece of string. You hold the string and make the yo-yo move up and down.

You need to practise to be good with a yo-yo.

zebra

A zebra is a wild animal. It looks like a horse with black-and-white stripes. Zebras live in Africa.

A zebra likes to eat grass.

zip

A zip joins two pieces of material together. Some clothes have a zip instead of buttons.

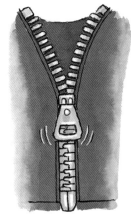

I like the zip on my coat because it is quick to do up.

The alphabet

 a is for apple

b is for banana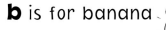

 c is for cake

d is for dog

 e is for elephant

f is for fairy

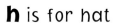 **g** is for gate

h is for hat

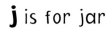 **i** is for ice cream

j is for jar

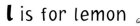 **k** is for kite

l is for lemon

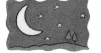 **m** is for moon

 n is for nest

o is for orange

 p is for pizza

q is for queen

 r is for rabbit

s is for sandcastle

 t is for teddy bear

u is for umbrella

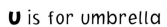 **v** is for vegetable

w is for witch

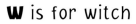 **x** is for xylophone

y is for yo-yo

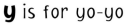 **z** is for zebra

Numbers

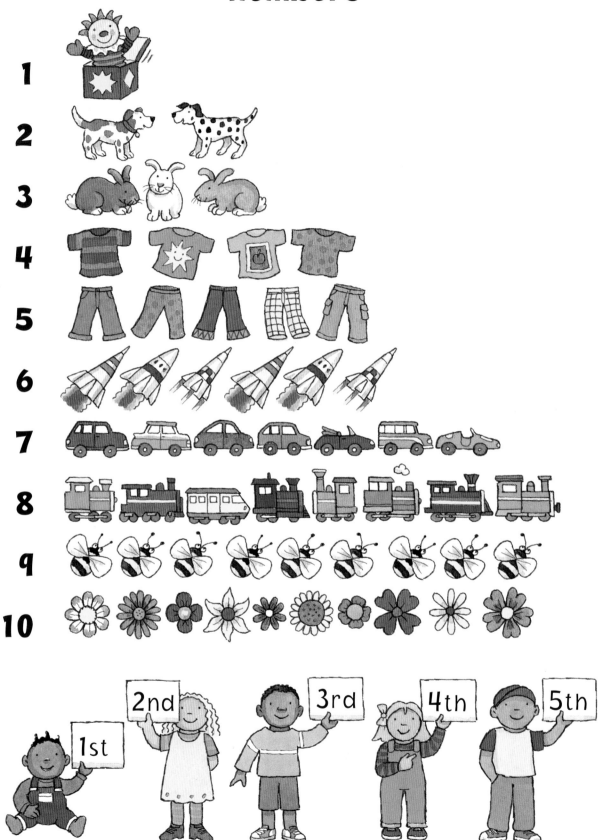

1

2

3

4

5

6

7

8

9

10

1st 2nd 3rd 4th 5th

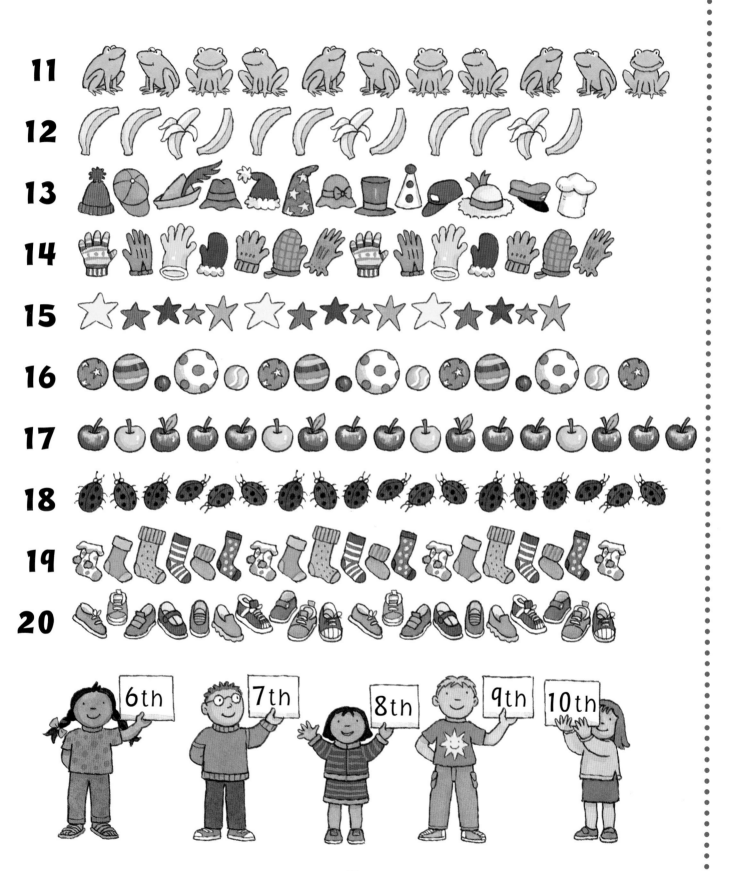

11

12

13

14

15

16

17

18

19

20

6th 7th 8th 9th 10th

Colours

 **green** frog

 **pink** pig

 **red** parrot

 **grey** elephant

 **orange** orang-utan

 **brown** monkey

 **white** sheep

 **black** cat

 **blue** butterfly

 **yellow** chick

 **purple** fish

Shapes

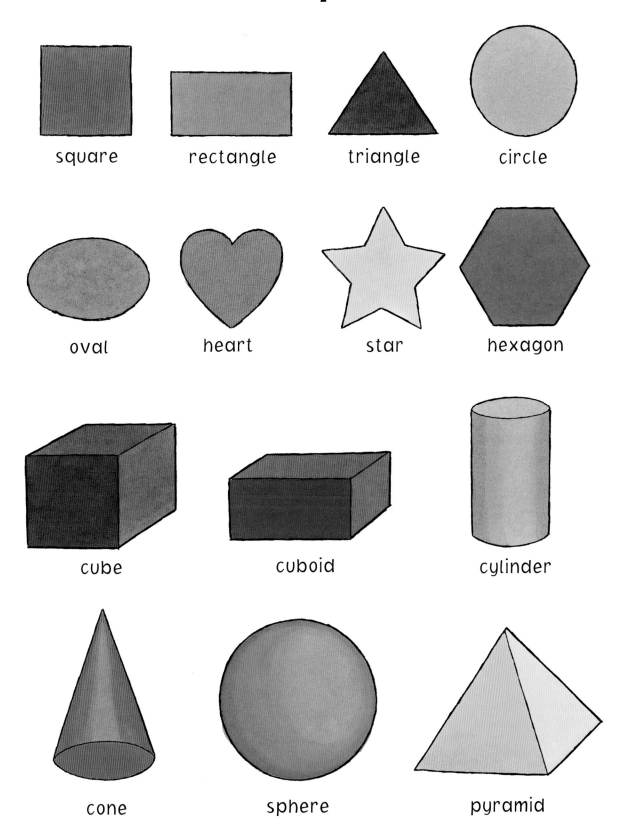

square

rectangle

triangle

circle

oval

heart

star

hexagon

cube

cuboid

cylinder

cone

sphere

pyramid

Opposites

awake

asleep

wet

dry

big

little

empty

full

fat

thin

old

new

open

shut

on

off

out

in

up

down

over

under

above

below

behind

in front of